To _____

From _____

Date _____

GOD CARES FOR YOU

PHOTOGRAPHY COPYRIGHT © 1997 BY VIRGINIA DIXON

TEXT COPYRIGHT © 1997 BY GARBORG'S HEART 'N HOME, INC.

DESIGN BY THURBER CREATIVE

PUBLISHED BY GARBORG'S HEART 'N HOME, INC.

P.O. BOX 20132, BLOOMINGTON, MN 55420

God
Cares For
You.

You are in the Beloved...therefore
infinitely dear to the Father, unspeakably
precious to Him. You are never, not for
one second, alone.

NORMAN DOWTY

The God who created, names, and
numbers the stars in the heavens also
numbers the hairs of my head.... He pays
attention to very big things and to very
small ones. What matters to me matters
to Him, and that changes my life.

ELISABETH ELLIOT

Have confidence in God's mercy, for
when you think He is a long way from
you, He is often quite near.

THOMAS À KEMPIS

Do you believe that God is near? He
wants you to. He wants you to know that
He is in the midst of your world.
Wherever you are as you read these
words, He is present.... And He is more
than near. He is active.

MAX LUCADO

My life is but a weaving
Between my Lord and me,
I cannot choose the colors
He worketh steadily.
Oftimes He weaveth sorrow,
And I in foolish pride
Forget He sees the upper
And I the underside.
Not till the loom is silent
And the shuttles cease to fly
Shall God unroll the canvas
And explain the reason why.
The dark threads are as needful
In the Weaver's skillful hand
As the threads of gold and silver
In the pattern He has planned.

I asked God for all things that I might enjoy life. He gave me life that I might enjoy all things.

If...you seek the Lord your God, you will find him if you look for him with all your heart and with all your soul.

DEUTERONOMY 4:29 NIV

God is every moment totally aware of
each one of us. Totally aware in intense
concentration and love.... No one passes
through any area of life, happy or tragic,
without the attention of God.

EUGENIA PRICE

God loves and cares for us, even to the
least event and smallest need of life.

HENRY EDWARD MANNING

When we call on God, He bends down
His ear to listen, as a father bends down
to listen to his little child.

ELIZABETH CHARLES

He is like a father to us, tender and
sympathetic.... For he knows we are but
dust, and that our days are few and brief,
like grass, like flowers, blown by the wind
and gone forever. But the loving kindness
of the Lord is from everlasting to
everlasting to those who reverence him.

PSALM 103:13-17 TLB

There is no need to plead that the love of God shall fill our hearts as though He were unwilling to fill us.... Love is pressing around us on all sides like air. Cease to resist it and instantly love takes possession.

AMY CARMICHAEL

God's heart is the most sensitive and tender of all. No act goes unnoticed, no matter how insignificant or small.

RICHARD FOSTER

God possesses infinite knowledg

His. At all times, eve.

I can realize that He knows, loves

and more than that

God is constantly takin

watching over m.

nd an awareness which is uniquely

n the midst of any type of suffering,

watches, understands,

He has a purpose. BILLY GRAHAM

cnowledge of me in love and.

for my good. J. I. PACKER

Your heavenly Father knows your needs.
He will always give you all you need
from day to day if you will make the
Kingdom of God your primary concern.
So don't be afraid, little flock.
For it gives your Father great happiness
to give you the Kingdom....
Your treasures there will
never disappear.

LUKE 12:30-33 TLB

God...will take care of you day and
night forever.

DR. NORMAN VINCENT PEALE

It is God to whom and with whom
we travel, and while He is the End of our
journey, He is also at every
stopping place.

ELISABETH ELLIOT

God will never, never, never let us down if
we have faith and put our trust in Him.
He will always look after us. So we must
cleave to Jesus. Our whole life must
simply be woven into Jesus.

MOTHER TERESA

God loves each one of us as if there were only one of us.

AUGUSTINE

May your roots go down deep into the soil of God's marvelous love; and may you be able to feel and understand, as all God's children should, how long, how wide, how deep, and how high his love really is; and to experience this love for yourselves, though it is so great that you will never see the end of it.

EPHESIANS 3:17-19 TLB

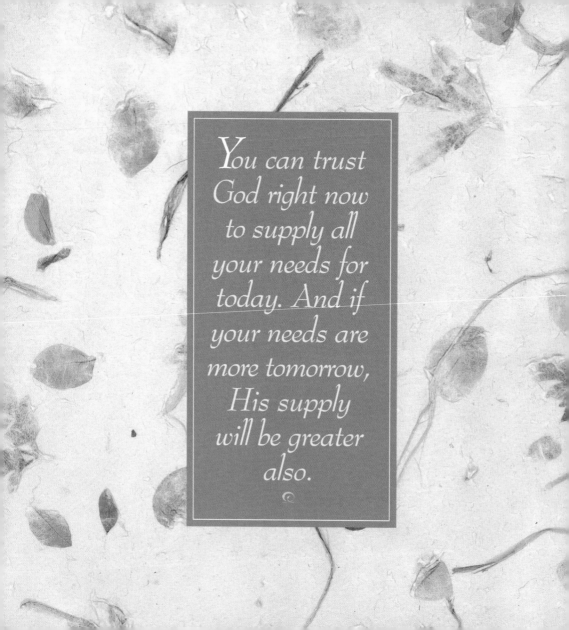

You can trust
God right now
to supply all
your needs for
today. And if
your needs are
more tomorrow,
His supply
will be greater
also.

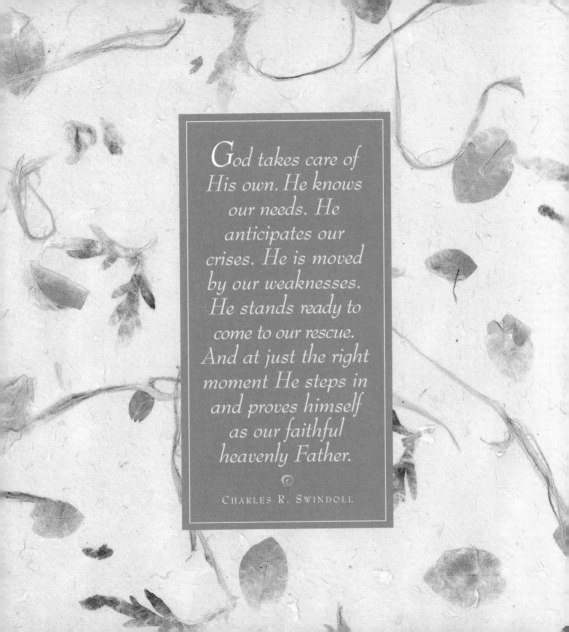

God takes care of His own. He knows our needs. He anticipates our crises. He is moved by our weaknesses. He stands ready to come to our rescue. And at just the right moment He steps in and proves himself as our faithful heavenly Father.

CHARLES R. SWINDOLL

The Lord's chief desire is to reveal himself

He gives you abundant grace

enjoying His presence. He touches you

more than ever, you are

He will keep in perfect peace all those

to the Lord! Trust in the Lord

is your everlasting strength.

to you and, in order for Him to do that,

The Lord gives you the experience of

His touch is so delightful that,

drawn inwardly to Him.
MADAME JEANNE GUYON

who trust in him, whose thoughts turn often

God always, for in the Lord Jehovah

AIAH 26:3,4 TLB

All God's glory and beauty come from within, and there He delights to dwell. His visits there are frequent, His conversation sweet, His comforts refreshing, His peace passing all understanding.

THOMAS À KEMPIS

God will never let you be shaken or moved from your place near His heart.

JONI EARECKSON TADA

We have been in God's thought from all eternity, and in His creative love, His attention never leaves us.

MICHAEL QUOIST

Nothing can separate you from His love, absolutely nothing.... God is enough for time, and God is enough for eternity. God is enough!

☙

HANNAH WHITALL SMITH

May the God of hope fill you with all joy and peace in believing, so that you may abound in hope.

☙

ROMANS 15:13 NKJV